How to use this

To test your vision simply open
the book and pass it to a friend.
Read the text from 1 metre and then ask
your friend to move one step
back and attempt to read again.

If you don't have a friend then you could
ask your partner, neighbour,
colleague or an obedient dog.
Or you could just prop the book up and
move back yourself. I probably should've
said that one first really.

Each eye chart is an anagram of a
person, place or thing associated with
the pandemic. If you are stuck then
have a look at the foot of the page for
help. If you are a smart arse and want to
make it harder then don't look at the
clue. To make it even harder spin
around on the spot and poke yourself in
the eye before looking at the puzzle.

Enjoy

B
JO
RNS
OONISH

2 words - person

C
ON
VIC
TANIA

1 word - thing

F

LO

UR

HUG

1 word - thing

4

I

TC

HYW

RIST

2 words - person

S

NO

RTING

TWEED

2 words - place

N
AC
HOCAT
MKT

2 words - person

O

ZO

OIQ

MU

2 words - thing

K

ER

RYW

OKES

2 words - thing

F

LE

ASOW

LTATTLER

3 words - thing

A
LI
ENIST
FOOLS

2 words - thing

M
RR
UB
EN

2 words - thing

C

ARN

IVOR

OUS

1 word - thing

S

TE

AMY

HO

2 words - saying

E

LV

ISS

AVE

2 words - saying

P

TE

ROCT

ETHHNS

3 words - saying

C

LO

DW

ONK

1 word - thing

B

UL

E

B

1 word - thing

M
IN
CED
PA

1 word - thing

S

AFE

SMA

CK

2 words - object

A
LLA
NSERV
IETTES

2 words - rule

A

DRI

ANTHO

LOGIST

HOWLER

3 words - agency

N
EAR
QUA
INT

1 word - thing

A
CCOL
ADING
INSIST

2 words - thing

E

LF

UXO

RIS

3 words - law

A
UTO
ELUTE
HOTPOT

5 words - scheme

C

ARP

ALS

FORCER

3 words - something that we did

A
NCE
STRA
LBARD

2 words - place

L

IL

ROOT

LETS

2 words - product

A

ERI

EDYS

LEXIC

2 words - something we were entitled to

E

VENT

FUL

CHATTER

3 words - phrase

T

HY

AHAB

DRIPPY

2 words - song

B

IN

GYAIR

FIELD

2 words - something we watched (a lot)

A
DR
IANNE
SHITS

2 words - something we used (a lot)

A
NN
YGI
PUBIC

2 words - We were told not to!

M
ET
RO
MOO

2 words - person

E

MS

WOT

TER

2 words - a rule

J
OC
KW
ISE

2 words - person

D
ELE
TESEX
PLAINS

3 words - heard during anagram 32

A

CTS

MERYL

FISTFIGHT

3 words - They're red, amber and green

E
URO
RIFT

2 words - the highest

H
U
N
WA

1 word - place

C
ON
TTACT
ICGRAN

2 words - people's movements

H

AI

RUN

KISS

2 words - person

M
OR
ON
IC

1 word - variant

A

NZ

ACE

ATERS

1 word - vaccine

A
CCR
AKALV
INPELT

2 words - Chief Scientific Adviser

T
IM
MY
UNI

1 word

A
RS
ONIST
SMIN

1 word - to do with the spread, also part of a car

A

IM

CAMP

YTOTS

1 word - showing no signs

G

ET

EVI

AN

1 word - test result

ANSWERS

1. Boris Johnson
2. Vaccination
3. Furlough
4. Chris Witty
5. Downing Street
6. Matt Hancock
7. Zoom Quiz
8. Key Workers
9. Lateral Flow Test
10. Self Isolation
11. R Number
12. Coronavirus
13. Stay Home
14. Protect the NHS
15. Save Lives

16. Lockdown

17. Bubble

18. Pandemic

19. Face Masks

20. Essential travel

21. World Heath Organisation

22. Quarantine

23. Social Distancing

24. Rule of Six

25. Eat out to help out

26. Clap for carers

27. Barnard Castle

28. Toilet rolls

29. Daily exercise

30. Flatten the curve

31. Happy Birthday

32. Daily Briefing

33. Hand Sanitiser

34. Panic Buying

35. Tom Moore

36. Two Metres
37. Joe Wicks
38. Next Slide Please
39. Traffic Light System
40. Tier Four
41. Wuhan
42. Contact Tracing
43. Rishi Sunak
44. Omicron
45. Astra Zeneca
46. Patrick Vallance
47. Immunity
48. Transmission
49. Asymptomatic
50. Negative

Dear Sir/Madam,

It is with regret/joy (delete as appropriate) that I am writing to you to inform you of my decision to resign from the position of...........................

I have been a loyal servant for for.....years/months/days and I like to think that I have always given 100% (adjust as appropriate) to the role. I have enjoyed working with you and it's not true what everyone else says about you (mostly).

I expect that this decision will come as a shock to you. Maybe you should take a seat and enjoy a nice, cold/warm/hard .... You may try to change my mind but please do not waste your time. This man/woman/gender fluid person is not for turning.

Okay, if you insist on forcing my hand I would consider withdrawing my resignation if you were to offer me a 20/50/100% pay rise, a company car and a 14 day, all inclusive holiday to Benidorm each year.

I would require you to respond to this request in the next 24 hours. If I do not hear from you I will withdraw my resignation withdrawal, if that makes sense.

I look forward to hearing from you,

Yours Sincerely/Kind Regards/Yours/Peace out/Much Love/It's been emotional.

Name

Resignation Template

Printed in Great Britain
by Amazon

13580801R00032